The Story of Flight

HELICOPTERS

Crabtree Publishing Company

www.crabtreebooks.com

PMB 16A, 350 Fifth Avenue,
Suite 3308
New York, NY 10118

612 Welland Avenue
St. Catharines, Ontario
L2M 5V6

Published in 2004 by
Crabtree Publishing Company

Coordinating editor: Ellen Rodger
Project editors: Sean Charlebois, Carrie Gleason
Production coordinator: Rose Gowsell

Created and Produced by
David West 🏃 Children's Books

Project Development, Design, and Concept
David West Children's Books:
Designer: Rob Shone
Editor: Gail Bushnell
Illustrators: James Field, Stephen Sweet & Ross Watton
(SGA), Gary Slater & Steve Weston (Specs Art), Alain
Salesse (Contact Jupiter), Alex Pang.
Picture Research: Carlotta Cooper

Photo Credits:
Abbreviations: t-top, m-middle, b-bottom, r-right,
l-left, c-center.

Front cover & page 18 - Rex Features. 6t, 8t & b, 11 -
The Culture Archive. 6b, 24b - Royal Air Force
Museum. 10, 13, 15t & b, 19, 24t, 29t - The Flight
Collection. 12, 17, 27t & b - Steen Media. 20 -
C.H.C. Helicopter Corporation. 21bl & br, 25 -
Corbis Images. 26 - Exec 162F Helicopter from
Rotorway International. 28, 29b - NASA.

06 05 04 03
10 9 8 7 6 5 4 3 2 1

Printed and bound in Dubai

Library of Congress Cataloging-in-Publication Data
Hansen, Ole Steen.
  Helicopters/ written by Ole Steen Hansen.
    p. cm. -- (The story of flight)
  Includes index.
  Contents: Lift and torque -- The first helicopters --Combat rescue --
The helicopter war -- Multi-role helicopters -- Over the battlefield --
Combat helicopters -- Over the sea -- Over the land -- Heavy lifters --
Small helicopters -- Into the future -- Spotters' guide.
  ISBN 0-7787-1208-7 (RLB : alk. paper) -- ISBN 0-7787-1224-9 (PB
: alk. paper)
  1. Helicopters--Juvenile literature. [1. Helicopters.] I. Title.
TL716.2.H36 2003
629.133'352--dc22
                                                    2003016003

The Story of Flight
HELICOPTERS

Ole Steen Hansen

 Crabtree Publishing Company
www.crabtreebooks.com

CONTENTS

THE CLIPPER OF THE CLOUDS
Science fiction writer Jules Verne wrote a book in 1886 called *The Clipper of the Clouds*. The ship in the book's title flew using 74 electric powered rotors. The ship was never built, but it inspired many future helicopter designers.

COMMUTER 'COPTERS
Helicopters can do jobs that no other aircraft can, like flying wealthy business people in and out of busy city centers.

INTRODUCTION

The idea of flying with rotors is almost as old as the idea of flying with wings. As early as the 1800s people started designing rotor winged aircraft. Eventually, after decades of trial and error, they created a helicopter that could actually fly. Designing and flying a helicopter is much more difficult than flying a fixed winged aircraft.

VERSATILITY

Fighting fires on dangerously steep hillsides is just one of the many tasks that helicopters are used for today.

LIFT AND TORQUE

PAUL CORNU
In 1907, French helicopter pioneer Paul Cornu designed a helicopter that lifted off the ground.

The early pioneers of helicopter flight faced two major problems. One problem was how to create enough lift. The other problem was called torque – a turning or twisting force that sends the helicopter in the opposite direction from the turning rotor.

It takes more engine power to lift an aircraft with a rotor than to lift one with wings. In the early 1900s, helicopters could not get off the ground. At the same time, fixed winged aircraft were flying across the English Channel.

Ellehammer's Helicopter
The two rotors on Ellehammer's helicopter were driven by **shafts**, one turning inside the other. The torque from one rotor counteracted the torque from the other. This two rotor system was tried again in the 1920s on other helicopters but did not work. Today, many helicopters use it to fly.

After many design failures, it seemed that rotor winged flight was an impossibility. Producing enough lift to bring a helicopter off the ground was just one challenge for designers. Torque meant that helicopters would rotate dangerously in circles. Helicopter designer Paul Cornu counteracted torque by having two rotors, one at each end of the aircraft. Danish inventor Jacob Ellehammer also experimented with two rotors. He placed one above the other. Both ideas worked and the helicopters lifted into the air without spinning, but they could not be controlled and eventually they were abandoned.

GOING AROUND IN CIRCLES

If a rotor is turning one way, the body of the helicopter will turn the other. The helicopter is heavier, so it will turn slower. A helicopter needs to counteract this torque to avoid spinning around and around. Having two main rotors is one way of solving the problem, but a small tail rotor has become the most widely used way of counteracting the torque from the main rotor.

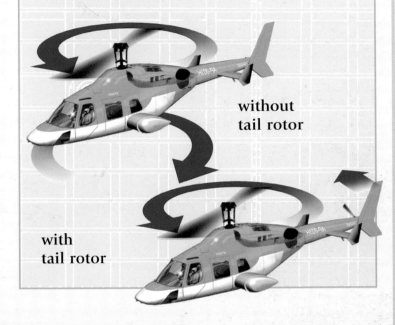

without tail rotor

with tail rotor

LIFT OFF

Paul Cornu's helicopter flew a few feet off the ground, but only for about 20 seconds. It was a great achievement, but it was not a practical flying machine. Cornu had absolutely no control over it.

THE FIRST HELICOPTERS

The first real helicopters flew shortly before World War II. The most important breakthrough in helicopter flight came in the United States when Russian emigrant and aircraft designer Igor Sikorsky invented the tail rotor.

The French designed Breguet-Doran Gyreoplane-Laboratoire flew for over an hour in the 1930s, but the work on this promising helicopter was stopped by World War II. The machine used two rotors, one on top of the other. In Germany, designers settled for two rotors on struts placed right and left of the helicopter to counteract torque. During World War II, Germany's plan to mass produce helicopters for its navy and army was stopped by **Allied** bombing. In the U.S., Igor Sikorsky tested the VS-300, which became the world's first tail rotor helicopter. Tail rotor helicopters are common today and even in the 1940s seemed to be the obvious solution to the helicopter flight problem.

FA 223 DRACHE
The German-designed Fa 223 was designed as a civilian **helicopter** in 1938. When the prototype was ready for testing in 1939, the German government decided to use it for the military. Allied bombing raids during World War II stopped work on the project. After the war, one Fa 223 was flown to England for testing. It was the first helicopter ever to cross the English Channel.

Hanna Reitsch and the Fw 61
The German Focke-Achgelis Fw 61 was the world's first easy to operate helicopter. German **aviatrix** Hanna Reitsch demonstrated how well the Fw 61 could be guided by flying it inside a big sports hall in 1938. Soon, the Fw 61 set a number of records, including flights up to an altitude of 11,244 feet (3,427 meters) and for a distance of 143 miles (230 kilometers).

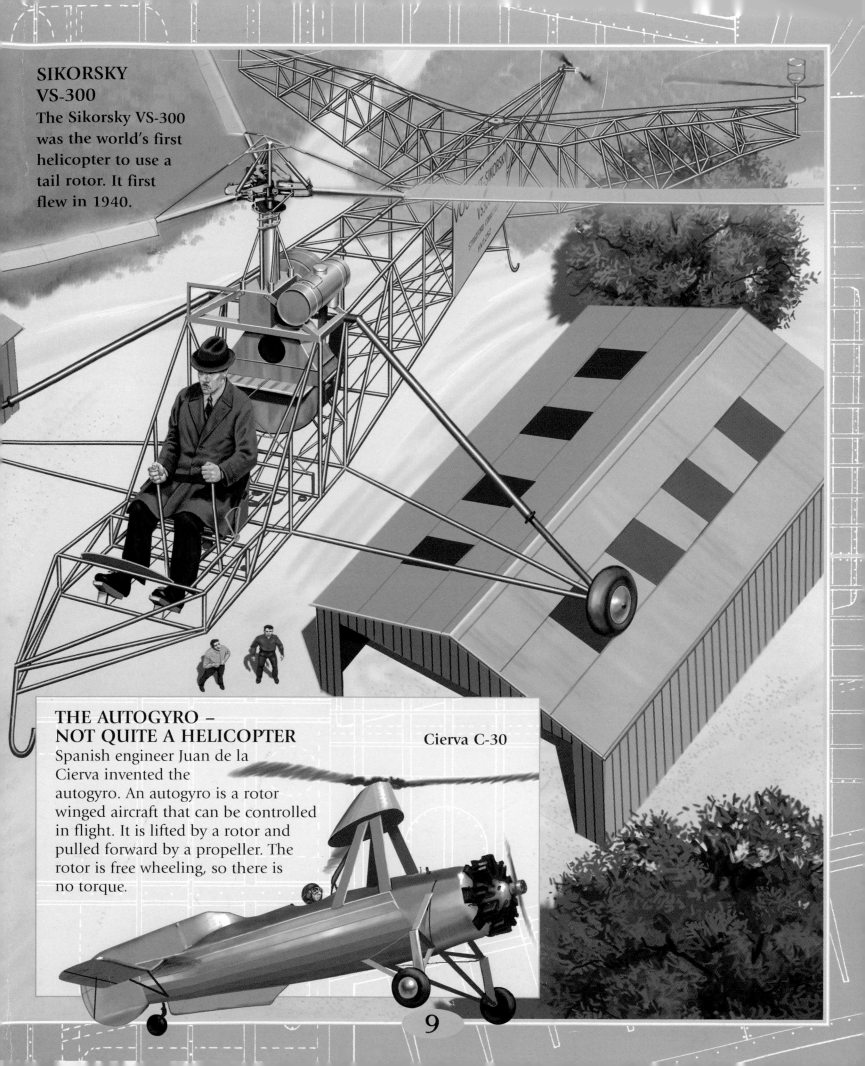

SIKORSKY VS-300

The Sikorsky VS-300 was the world's first helicopter to use a tail rotor. It first flew in 1940.

THE AUTOGYRO – NOT QUITE A HELICOPTER

Cierva C-30

Spanish engineer Juan de la Cierva invented the autogyro. An autogyro is a rotor winged aircraft that can be controlled in flight. It is lifted by a rotor and pulled forward by a propeller. The rotor is free wheeling, so there is no torque.

COMBAT RESCUE

During the Korean War (1950–53) helicopters were used on a large scale for the first time. They flew troops into battle and they evacuated the wounded from the front lines.

SIKORSKY S-55
The S-55 was used in Korea and later in more than 30 air forces around the world. In Britain, it was called the Westland Whirlwind.

MERCY MISSIONS
A total of 30,000 wounded were flown to the MASHs in Korea. Bell 47s were one of the helicopters used.

Helicopters were used by the United States armed forces to quickly move wounded soldiers from the front to Mobile Army Surgical Hospitals (MASHs) just outside the front. Korea's many mountains made it difficult to land planes or drive vehicles to bring the wounded to hospitals. The wounded needed to be evacuated quickly so helicopters were used. Helicopters were still in the early stages of development and had a very limited lifting capacity, but they could lift **litters** with wounded soldiers sometimes strapped to the outside. Wounded soldiers who needed blood transfusions during the flight were given blood through tubes that ran through holes cut in the fuselage, or body, of the helicopter.

Valérie Andreé
The Hiller HH-1 was used to evacuate wounded during the 1945–54 war in **Indochina**, where French soldiers fought against **Communist** Vietnamese guerrillas who wanted to be free of **colonial rule**. French doctor and pilot, Valérie Andreé, flew over 120 missions in a Hiller HH-1, saving 165 French soldiers.

TANDEM ROTORS
Tandem Rotor helicopters, nicknamed "flying bananas," were developed in the late 1940s and early '50s. At the time they were the world's largest helicopters. The H-21 first flew during the Korean War. It became a widely used military transport helicopter in the U.S., Canada, France, Germany, and Japan.

H-21C Shawnee
"Flying Banana"

THE HELICOPTER WAR

The usefulness of helicopters in battle was already proven during the war in Korea. During the war in Vietnam (early 1960s–1975), helicopters were used in larger numbers than ever before or since.

In Vietnam, helicopters were used in many roles. Bell Huey helicopters flew as "slicks" carrying soldiers into battle in rice paddies or jungle clearings.

Hughes OH-6 Cayuse
Many types of helicopters used in Vietnam are still flying with military and civilian operators in various countries. One is the Hughes OH-6 seen here flying with the Danish Army in 2002. In Vietnam, OH-6s flew low over the treetops and were often in close combat with enemy ground troops only a few feet (or meters) below.

COBRA ATTACK
The HueyCobra was a slimmed down Huey with a narrow fuselage. It attacked targets with rockets and heavy machine guns.

The job was very risky since the helicopters had little protection against enemy gunners hiding in tree lines or the tropical rainforest. Support for rescue slicks was provided by other Huey helicopters armed with machine guns and rockets. They were called "guns." Unarmed Dustoff Hueys carrying **Red Cross** markings evacuated the dead and wounded soldiers. The U.S. forces needed more specialized helicopters to perform some functions such as supporting ground troops. The HueyCobra had a powerful engine and wide rotor blades, which gave it a much higher top speed. Heavily armed, it was the first true helicopter gunship designed to support other helicopters and troops on the ground.

SIKORSKY H-53 "JOLLY GREEN GIANT"
"Jolly Green Giants" were large rescue helicopters. They had self-sealing fuel tanks and armor plating to protect them against enemy fire. They picked up pilots shot down behind enemy lines and flew them back to safety.

BELL UH-1 HUEY IROQUOIS
More than any other type of helicopter, the Huey became associated with the Vietnam War. It turned U.S. Army units into airborne **cavalry**. On many days more than 2,000 Hueys would be flying over Vietnam. About 3,305 Hueys were lost in the war and 2,709 aircrew and soldiers died flying in them.

SPLASH-DOWN PICK-UP
The S-61 is a highly efficient Search and Rescue (SAR) helicopter. S-61s were also used to pick up the astronauts when their spacecraft landed in the sea in the 1960s and '70s.

POWER PLANT
Early helicopters were powered by **piston engines**, like almost all aircraft up until the end of World War II. The S-61 has two turbine, or jet, engines each producing about 1,300 horsepower. Turbine engines produce more power for their weight, vibrate less, and have fewer mechanical troubles.

MULTI-ROLE HELICOPTERS

A large dependable helicopter can be equipped to perform many roles. One helicopter that has proven this over and over again is the Sikorsky S-61. Through more than four decades, the Sikorsky S-61 has been a large part of the history of flight.

The S-61 first flew in 1959 as an anti-submarine helicopter for the U.S. Navy. It was designed to land at sea and therefore has a boat-shaped hull and outrigger floats to balance it in the water. Salt water is not good for the metal structures so S-61s seldom actually land in water. In its Anti-Submarine Warfare (ASW) role the S-61 was equipped with sensors to detect submarines and weapons to destroy them. Another version of the helicopter is the H-3 used for anti-drug patrols by the U.S. Coast Guard. "Marine 1," the helicopter of the President of the United States, is an H-3. Sikorsky-61s are flown in Canada, Argentina, Brazil, Denmark, Norway, Germany, Egypt, India, and Japan.

CIVIL WORK
Several companies around the world have operated S-61s as civilian helicopters. For civilian use, the helicopters have a longer fuselage to allow for more seats. This one is flying with Air Greenland.

Super Frelon
The French Super Frelon helicopter is slightly larger than the S-61. It is another example of a multi-use helicopter. Super Frelons have been used for transporting people in the off-shore oil industry, to fight fires, and in various military roles including evacuation of wounded soldiers and anti-submarine warfare.

Tail rotor   Drive shaft   Rotor head   Turbine engines

NAVY 66

Sikorsky S-61

GROUND HUGGING

Even a heavily armed McDonnell Douglas AH-64A Apache helicopter risks being shot down. The Apache flies low, which means it also has to fly slower to avoid hitting objects. Staying low also gives it the best chance of survival.

Seeing in the Dark

At night, pilots often wear either image intensifier or infra-red night vision goggles. The goggles give pilots a two dimensional image, so a lot of training is needed to use them. The distance to a tree, for example, has to be judged by the size of it. It becomes difficult if you do not know whether the tree is large or small.

OVER THE BATTLEFIELD

Helicopters are used by the armed forces of most nations to provide firepower on the battlefield. Surviving in combat warfare calls for special flying skills and tactics.

Helicopters are slower than jets and therefore easier to shoot down. Helicopters fly very low in a combat zone. A group of helicopters wind their way forward in a loose formation, moving fast and making sure nobody flies over the same spot where another has just been. If an enemy soldier is somewhere below, the first helicopter will alert the soldier, who will be ready to fire at the next. Near the front line, transport helicopters deliver their loads, while combat helicopters take up **ambush** positions behind buildings, rocks, or trees. From here they can appear suddenly and attack the enemy before the enemy has time to shoot them down.

FENNEC FORMATION
Fennec helicopters fight tanks. Here they are practising tight formation flying at an altitude of 1,000 feet (305 meters). In combat, this would be dangerous. Instead, they fly in a loose formation at 10 feet (3 meters), to avoid detection.

SEEING WITHOUT BEING SEEN
While hiding behind a line of trees, a Bell OH-58D helicopter uses its **mast mounted sight** to look for targets. The mast has tv cameras to give the crew pictures, infra-red cameras to see in the dark, and lasers to point out the targets. Other helicopters carry the weapons and attack the enemy.

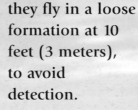

COMBAT HELICOPTERS

The Vietnam War meant the creation of more combat helicopters. The design of these helicopters began in the late 1960s and early 1970s and continues today. Combat helicopters are fast, heavily armed, and dangerous to enemies on the battlefield.

Modern combat helicopters have many receivers and a **jammer** that helps the crew detect and jam enemy radars and radar controlled missiles. Crew protection includes crash resistant fuel systems that lessen the risk of fire in case of a crash.

THE CREW
Most attack helicopters are flown by a pilot and a co-pilot/gunner. The gunner operates a machine-gun mounted in a turret under the nose.

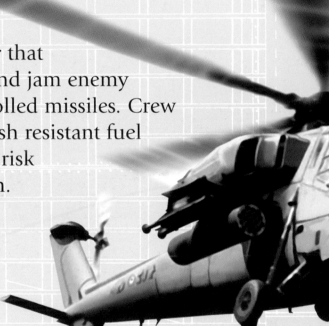

AGUSTA A129 MANGUSTA
Country: Italy
Length: 40 ft (12.2 m)
Rotor diameter: 38 ft 9 in (11.8 m)
Speed: 162 mph (261 km/h)

Hovering

Forward flight

Backward flight

MOVING
All helicopters tilt their rotors to fly forward, backward, or to the sides. If a fast acceleration is required the helicopter will lower its nose to the rotor to help pull it forward faster. Combat helicopters have rotors that make it possible for them to turn and maneuver very fast.

WESTLAND/AEROSPATIALE LYNX
Country: Great Britain, France
Length: 38 ft 3 in (11.7 m)
Rotor diameter: 42 ft (12.8 m)
Speed: 207 mph (333 km/h)

Flares
A Chinook fires flares to fool heat seeking missiles fired by an enemy. Heat seeking missiles are a danger to helicopters flying over the battlefield. Hot flares fool the missiles into "thinking" that the flares are a helicopter's hot engine. Instead of hitting their target, the missiles hit the flares.

The fuselage structure will collapse in a way that gives the crew the best possible chance of survival. There is no guarantee of survival in combat. A combat helicopter carries many different kinds of weapons from machine-guns, to rockets and anti tank missiles, all used to attack targets on the ground. The combat helicopter may also carry air-to-air missiles to fight enemy jets or helicopters. In the **Soviet Union**, combat helicopters were designed to operate in formation with tanks on the ground.

MIL MI-28 "HAVOC"
Country: Soviet Union
Length: 56 ft 7 in (17.3 m)
Rotor diameter: 55 ft 3 in (16.9 m)
Speed: 231 mph (372 km/h)

OVER THE SEA

The helicopter's ability to land on small platforms on oil rigs or ships makes it very useful at sea. By hovering almost motionless over a spot, a helicopter can also rescue people in danger without ever needing to land.

Oil companies spend a lot of money drilling for oil in the world's oceans. They set up large platforms with rigs in the oceans where crews of oil workers live and work for weeks at a time. Helicopters are the most convenient option for transporting crews out to these platforms, saving the crew much longer trips in ships. When important equipment on the platform breaks down, it is very costly if it brings oil production to a standstill. It does not matter that it is cheaper to sail the spare part out to the rig. A helicopter will usually be given the job of flying the part out, as quickly as possible. Offshore helicopter operations are big business. The Canadian CHC Helicopter Service has more than 300 helicopters operating in 23 different countries. The majority of these are used by the offshore oil industry.

LANDING ON SHIPS

Landing on a ship's helicopter platform is not difficult in calm seas. It is very difficult in stormy weather with enormous waves. How do pilots land on a platform that moves that much? The trick is to fly in formation with the ship, finding the ship's rhythm as it goes up and down between waves. The helicopter can then land between waves.

THE COAST GUARD

The U.S. Coast Guard flies helicopters over the waters around the U.S. They use HH-65A Dauphins for search and rescue work. Dauphins fly from shore bases and from small ships.

Sea Rescue

Rescues from sinking ships in stormy weather are dangerous. The rescuer on the winch being lowered risks hitting the ship. Often there is the threat of fire. A rescue operation can last for hours, so the crew also has to keep an eye on the fuel used. This CHC rescue helicopter is approaching the Ikan Tanda ship to help the crew.

OIL RIG RENDEZVOUS

A Super Puma helicopter flies crew members out to an oil platform. Some helicopters also fly operations between the various oil rigs in an oil field. These helicopters are often kept on the rigs and fly only from rig to rig.

AP-001

AP-001

OVER THE LAND

Transporting people in mountain regions, checking power lines, evacuating victims from highway accidents, filming sporting events, or simply taking people on pleasure flights is all in a day's work for helicopter crews flying over land.

Flying low and slow along power lines is very dangerous in a fixed-winged airplane, but it is perfectly safe in a helicopter. The same can be said about flying close enough to shoot television footage during cycling races.

FIRE FIGHTER
The little Kaman HH-43 Huskie was used for fighting fires caused by aircraft crashes, often arriving on the scene before ground vehicles. It carried up to two fire fighters and had fire retardant under the cabin.

Police Patrol
Police forces use helicopters for traffic control. They are also used to search for missing or wanted persons. Large areas, such as forests or marshland, can be inspected quickly. An experienced helicopter observer can immediately spot things that do not fit into the natural surroundings. Sometimes criminals are caught by helicopter crews. The MBB BO 105 CB helicopter is flown by the German police.

AIR AMBULANCE

Helicopter ambulances are equipped with life saving equipment, and often have an emergency medical technician (EMT) as a crew member. People with serious injuries from ski or traffic accidents are picked up quickly and flown to hospital. The flying ambulance can land right on the site of the accident, saving both time and lives.

BELL 222

BOMBING SNOW

Avalanches are dangerous to ski resorts and roads. To reduce the risk and damage done, helicopters drop explosives on avalanche-prone mountainsides. The explosives start avalanches in a controlled way.

Helicopters fly people into mountain regions both for fun and out of necessity. Heli-skiing is an exciting and popular mountain sport. In North America, Asia, and Europe, companies offer vacations where you are flown out by helicopter and set down in high back-country mountain terrain. Skiing in these surroundings is breathtaking, but certainly not for beginners. If skiers, or other tourists, are injured in the mountains, helicopters are also used to bring them out again. If a search is necessary, helicopters sometimes fly alongside rescue dogs to locate people who need help.

23

HEAVY LIFTERS

Cargo planes are faster and can haul a heavier load, but large helicopters can land everywhere to deliver loads. Helicopters that can lift heavy loads are often used by the military.

Fast movement of troops and equipment is important to surprise the enemy on the battlefield. "Heavy lift" helicopters place troops and heavy guns where the enemy least expects them.

MI-26 "HALO"

The Russian Mil Mi-26 is the world's largest helicopter. It can carry a load of 20 tons. In Italy, two are used for fire fighting and can carry 2,600 gallons (10,000 liters) of water in two external baskets.

Vertol HUP H-25

The H-25 of the 1950s was an early "heavy lifter." By today's standards it carried a light load. The two rotors at each end of the helicopter meant the load could be placed almost anywhere inside. With a single rotor helicopter, the load has to be placed so it does not change the balance of the aircraft.

Small, heavily armed units can cut an enemy supply route, attack key targets, and create confusion. When required, the helicopters can pick up the units and fly them out again. Heavy lifters are also used for fire fighting when not at war. Hot and dry summers bring wildfires in forests and plains all over the world. The intense heat and winds mean it is very difficult for firefighters on the ground to stop the fires. Helicopters can load up, take off, and land quickly and are perfect for fighting these fires.

SUPER STALLION

The Sikorsky CH-53E Super Stallion can lift 35,926 pounds (16,330 kg) in a sling hanging under the helicopter. The MH-53J Pave Low III version seen here has electronic equipment that allows it to go undetected into enemy territory.

FLYING CRANES

The Sikorsky CH-54 Tarhe "Skycrane" was designed in the 1960s for hauling big guns, field hospital containers, and other heavy loads. Today it is used for fire fighting in Australia. The Skycrane has fire fighting equipment fitted and has helped to stop many fires.

Sikorsky
S-64 Tarhe
"Skycrane"

BOEING VERTOL CH-47 CHINOOK

Chinooks were already being used in the 1960s during the Vietnam War. This versatile helicopter was also used in the war in Iraq in 2003. It can carry more than 40 troops along with their equipment.

SMALL HELICOPTERS

Some non-military helicopters are not very big, but they can perform some big stunts. Helicopter companies now make kits for building your own helicopters, which you can fly to work, use for pleasure flights, or even break records with.

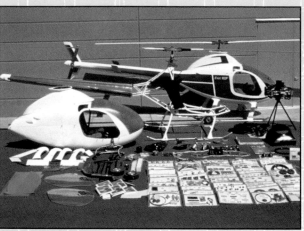

The Robinson R22 helicopter was designed because company founder Frank Robinson had a dream of producing a small, light helicopter for private flights.

HELICOPTER KITS

From a kit you can build a helicopter, such as these RotorWay Exec 162Fs, in your own garage. Even with a good kit it takes hundreds of hours. The finished helicopter is also more demanding to fly than most home built aircraft. Once finished, the pilot has the unique experience of flying a helicopter that they've built themselves!

ROTORWAY JAVELIN

The 1961 Javelin was RotorWay's first attempt at building a small helicopter. It was never successful, but eventually led the way for the Exec, a popular DIY helicopter today.

ULTRASPORT 496

Length: 19 ft 2 in (5.8 m)

Rotor diameter: 22 ft 9 in (7 m)

Speed: 91 mph (146 km/h)

ROBINSON R22

Length: 20 ft 5 in (6.3 m)
Rotor diameter:
25 ft (7.7 m)
Speed: 110 mph
(177 km/h)

SCHWEIZER 300C

Length: 22 ft 1 in (6.8 m)
Rotor diameter:
26 ft 8 in (8.2 m)
Speed: 92 mph (148 km/h)

SMALL IS BEAUTIFUL

More than 3,300 R22s have been sold worldwide. An R22 pilot once said: "Flying small helicopters is great fun. You can land everywhere and the feeling of freedom is unparalleled."

Why drive through traffic jams to your office if you can fly? The idea of everybody flying to their office skyscrapers may not be practical since traffic jams in the air would be the result. The two seat Robinson R22 has turned out to be very popular with private pilots. Some people dream of building their own helicopter. One way to do this is build from a kit like the RotorWay Exec. This helicopter began as a dream to produce a light helicopter for private users. Now, more than 600 kits have been sold worldwide.

ROTORWAY EXEC

Length:
21 ft 10 in (6.7 m)
Rotor diameter:
24 ft 6 in (7.6 m)
Speed:
115 mph
(184 km/h)

INTO THE FUTURE

A helicopter's rotor is good for taking off and landing vertically, but when flying from A to B and carrying a load of passengers or cargo, a fixed-winged aircraft will be cheaper, faster, and probably less noisy.

HALF AND HALF

The Bell XV-15 was a research aircraft flown in the early 1980s. It was the forerunner of today's V-22 Osprey. Both prop-rotors can be powered by just one of the engines, otherwise the aircraft would be in trouble if one engine failed.

VTDP

In 2000, Piasecki Aircraft received a U.S. Navy contract to develop a Vectored Thrust Ducted Propeller (VTDP) compound helicopter. This is a helicopter with small wings that will provide some of the lift in flight. This put less strain on the rotor. The VTDP helicopter may therefore fly faster or more economically at lower speed. The VTDP helicopter also has a fan at the tail to help push the helicopter forward. This project may actually change the appearance of future helicopters.

VTDP version of a Bell Huey Cobra

The idea of combining the advantages of vertical take-off using a rotor, like a helicopter, with economical cruising using wings, like an airplane, is not new. In the late 1950s the Fairey Rotodyne was an attempt to build an airliner along these lines. Today, the VTDP project has small, stubby wings and a fan in the tail that makes it partly a fixed-winged aircraft.

The V-22 Osprey is also a "half and half." When taking off, the prop-rotors lift the aircraft like a helicopter. They are then tilted to pull the Osprey forward like big propellers, while the wing lifts it. Traditional helicopters are also being constantly updated. The new EH-101 has heated rotor blades and air intakes to prevent ice forming. It can fly its Search and Rescue (SAR) missions in icy conditions that would have kept older SAR helicopters grounded.

WESTLAND AGUSTA EH-101
The EH-101 is a multi-role helicopter used both as a transport and SAR aircraft.

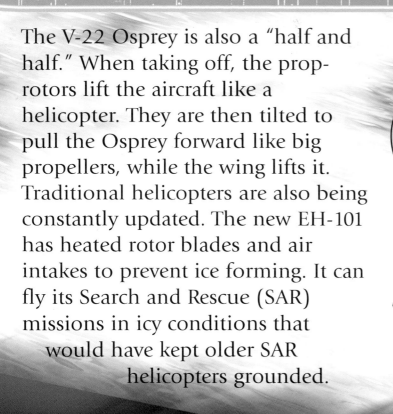

POWER BLADES
Small, unmanned fighting helicopters have the advantage that no pilot is at risk in combat. On the Boeing Dragonfly the rotor is used for take off while it is locked and then doubles as a wing during flight. The rotor is not turned by a gearbox as on a traditional helicopter. In hover mode, the jet exhaust is sent through the blades and out through nozzles in the tips which turns the rotor.

X Wings
   The X-wing was an U.S.-made research project that tried to combine the benefits of the helicopter with that of a fixed-wing aircraft. The X-wing could take off vertically. The rotor could then be locked and used as ordinary wings for fast forward flight when it was powered by two jet engines. Lack of funding ended the project in 1988. Today, unmanned helicopters are developed the same way.

SPOTTERS' GUIDE

CORNU HELICOPTER
Country: France
Length: 20 ft 2 in
(6.2 m)
Rotor diameter:
19 ft 6 in (6 m) each

Early helicopters could lift off the ground, but only during World War II (1939–1945) did it become possible to control helicopters in flight. The evolution of the helicopter was much slower than the evolution of the fixed-winged aircraft. Since World War II, very efficient helicopters – large and small, civilian and military, have been designed for many different tasks.

BELL MODEL 47 SIOUX
Country: U.S.A.
Length: 32 ft 7 in (9.9 m)
Rotor diameter: 37 ft 1 in (11.3 m)
Speed: 105 mph (169 km/h)

SIKORSKY VS-300
Country: U.S.A.
Length: 27 ft 7 in (8.5 m)
Rotor diameter: 29 ft 6 in (9.1 m)
Speed: 50 mph (80 km/h)

BELL MODEL 204 IROQUOIS (UH-1 HUEY)
Country: U.S.A.
Length: 40 ft 4 in (12.3 m)
Rotor diameter: 48 ft (14.6 m)
Speed: 120 mph (193 km/h)

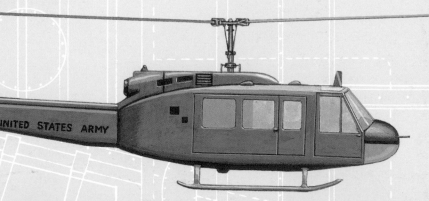

AEROSPATIALE SA 330 SUPER PUMA
Country: France
Length: 46 ft 1 in (14 m)
Rotor diameter: 49 ft 2 in (15 m)
Speed: 174 mph (280 km/h)

BELL MODEL 206 JET RANGER
Country: U.S.A.
Length: 31 ft 2 in (9.5 m)
Rotor diameter: 33 ft 4 in (10.1 m)
Speed: 140 mph (225 km/h)

BOEING VERTOL CH-47 CHINOOK
Country: U.S.A.
Length: 51 ft (15.5 m)
Rotor diameter: 60 ft (18.3 m) each
Speed: 190 mph (306 km/h)

BELL MODEL 209 HUEYCOBRA
Country: U.S.A.
Length: 44 ft 5 in (13.5 m)
Rotor diameter: 44 ft (13.4 m)
Speed: 219 mph (352 km/h)

MCDONNELL DOUGLAS AH-64 APACHE
Country: U.S.A.
Length: 48 ft 3 in (14.6 m)
Rotor diameter: 48 ft (14.6 m)
Speed: 230 mph (365 km/h)

INDEX

GLOSSARY

ALLIED Joined in an alliance or agreement to help each other. The Allies during World War II included Britain, France, the U.S.A., and the U.S.S.R.

AMBUSH A sudden attack on an enemy made from a hidden position.

AVIATRIX A female pilot.

CAVALRY A mobile army unit using light armor.

CIVILIAN A person who is not in the military.

COLONIAL RULE The control or rule by one nation over a foriegn country or dependancy.

COMMUNIST A government system in which the state plans and controls the economy, and owns all of its natural resources.

FRONT LINE Troops at the front of a war.

INDOCHINA A peninsula of southeast Asia which includes Vietnam, Laos, Cambodia, Thailand, Burma, and parts of Malaysia. The war in Indochina took place mostly in Vietnam.

JAMMER An electronic instrument that is used to prevent the clear reception of broadcast signals or messages.

KOREAN WAR A war between North Korea aided by China, and South Korea aided by United Nations forces that were mostly U.S. troops.

LITTER A carrier used for transporting wounded soldiers.

MAST MOUNTED SIGHT A viewer that is attached to the helicopter top.

OIL RIG A structure from which crude oil is drilled from the ground.

PISTON ENGINE A solid cylinder that fits into a larger one and moves under fluid pressure.

PROTOTYPE The original model.

RED CROSS An organization that cares for the wounded, sick, or homeless, during wartime. A Red Cross marking, or symbol, is a red cross set on a white background.

ROTOR A group of rotating airfoils.

SHAFTS A long cylindrical bar that transmits power to an engine.

SOVIET UNION The Union of Soviet Socialist Republics. A group of countries that were under communist rule from 1922–1991.